Letters to Love

Poetry & Photography Collection

Monique L. DeSargant

ISBN – 978-1-0878-9586-4

10 9 8 7 6 5 4 3 2-

LCCN:

Book Cover Images: Cincinart & Shangarey/stock.adobe.com
Front & Back Book Cover Designs: Monique L. DeSargant

Author Contact:
Letters2Love.mld@gmail.com

EMPIRE PUBLISHING
www.empirebookpublishing.com

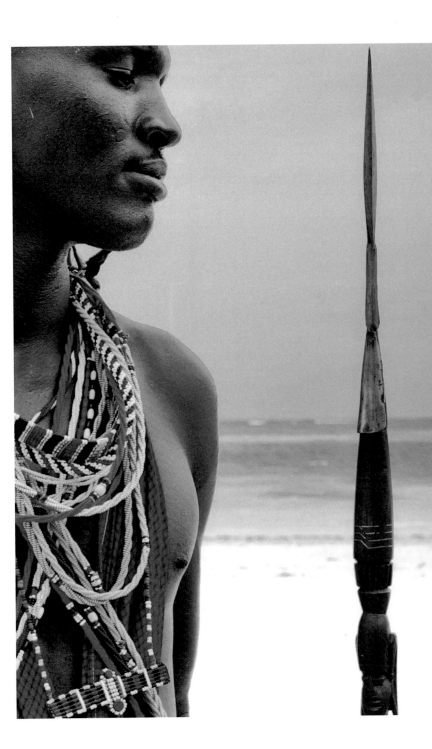

Table of Contents

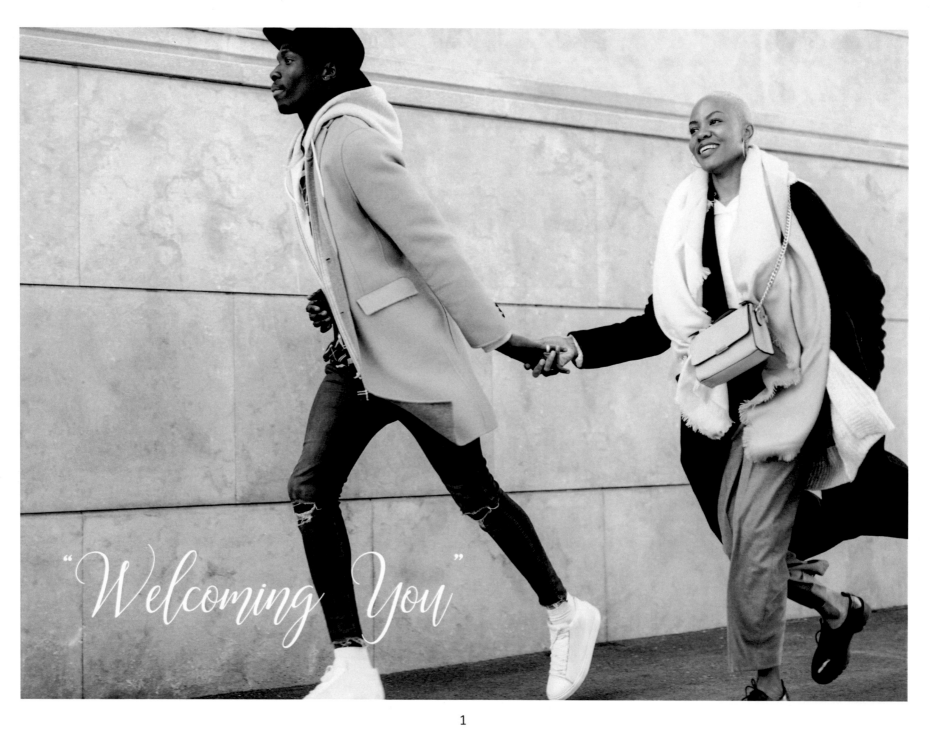

"Welcoming You"

"Welcoming You"

Love

You inspire me

You excite me

The spontaneous burst of joy when you laugh delights me

The mere presence of you without touch only site

Entertains my gazing eyes so politely

Golden Symmetry

You are honeyed beautifully from head to toe

Balanced, intelligent, kind-hearted

And the star of my show

Looking from a far

I sense composure, a caring and fare heart

Cultivation, consideration, and fascinating conversations

I am amused

And overwhelmed with your vivacity

Incredible flavor and alluring energy

Beautiful mind

Come with me

My arms are open, honest, and sugary

I welcome you on this spiritual journey through

Letters to Love

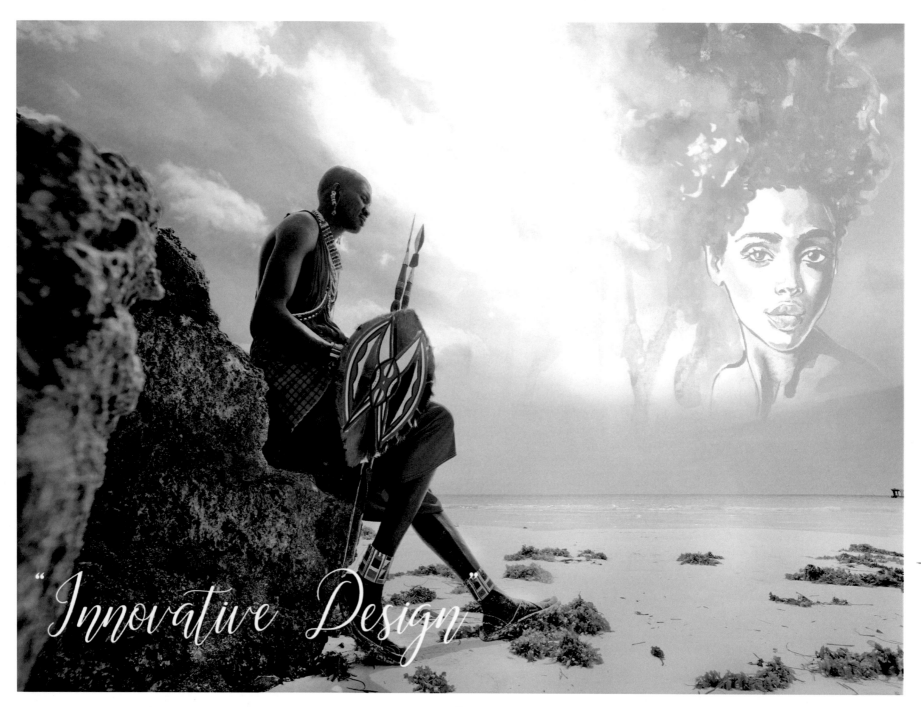

"Innovative Design"

"Innovative Design"

Ivory, lipstick red and honey hues remain vivid in color as though just painted today. My painting shines within like the sparkle of sunlight over a body of water. A fine creation, resting gently in my heart like the dew in the morning. My life began to change the moment I saw this painting. At first, I was overwhelmed, then, maybe just too excited. Now, my soul marinates passionately for one particular work of art. Unforgettable, preserved, unique and sweet like my Grandmothers antiques. No copy or duplication can compare or even compete. My painting is authentic, pure, blessed and sits in a gallery of its own. Colors, oils, texture, and canvas complexions are so tantalizing and distinct. This connection was meant and set before my eyes to study, grow, understand, and admire, beauty, strength, wit, visual and mental complexity. I believe this content of style is a masterpiece, I want to know more. Depth speaks through texture, and with one touch glyptic intensity is transferred. Like wine, the taste matures and gets finer with time, and through experience wisdom is redefined. My painting has no frame, deep and infinite space still remains. Faith without work is nothing, so I patiently create and pray for change.

Respect, Peace, Love, Patience, then Serenity

Eyes are the soul

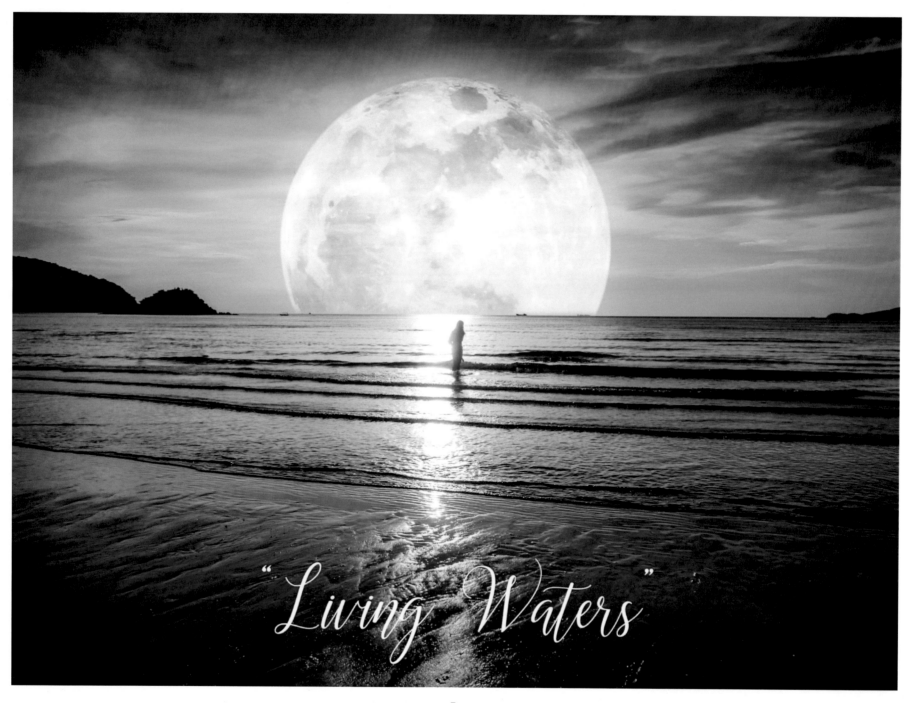

"Living Waters"

"Living Waters"

You are my sensual abyss, my spiritual realm, a safe place, and my heaven. Wet, comfortable, bluish and serene, your natural elegant agility delights my heart ever 'so politely. Warm, then cold when need be. Every splash, wave and tide satisfy my soul entirely. Your mental seduction revitalizes and fuels my conscious and subconscious mind with pleasant emotions and valuable nutrients. Positivity dominates, then eliminates all else not in favor of such a connection. My heart gets eager at times and wants to flow, follow, and intertwine with your currents, but spiritual advice says, "slowly, slowly." "Spring will come, waters will calm, direction will change, and emotions will eventually return to open waters." At night, I swim to the top, above sea, just to watch the moonlight caress and dance with your body. Love one if I were the moon clouds would be very few. So, night and day, I can hold you closer than anyone before, while slow dancing to the sounds of our gentle whispers. These feelings I've held close through continuous travel across the deepest seas. A dolphin is what I am, and complete pleasure is what I feel when in your presence. The embrace of you is what my heart desires. My soul recognized you that first day and it won't let go.

Living Waters, let it flow.

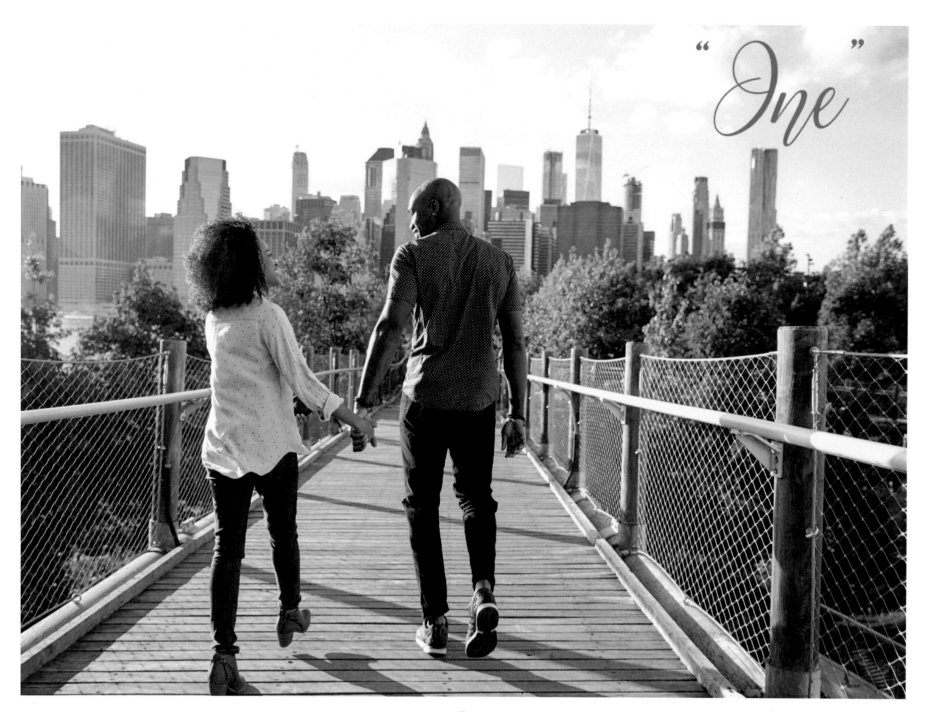

"*One*"

"One"

One thought, one look, one glance, one step towards love is the plan. One touch, one word, one love with the essence stronger than any other soul living amidst our Motherland. Once, I saw you dance, once we held hands. Lovie, I need to feel that way again! One dream into many, the first began at the far end of a long hallway, which lead to a set of stairs, then over a grassy hill, and across the hot African desert sands. Then finally, at the top of a bridge over waters in a foreign land you and I stand. Can we hang out or stay in, rent movies, cook dinner or order in? Take a stroll around the park in the dark, look over the city from Anthem Hills or a mountaintop? Sweetie let me pull you closer to my heart. Trips out of town, around town, up and down the trails of Red Rock and desert ground. Let's be spontaneous, touch again, laugh again and talk with our hands. Then, for the first time tell me how you really feel. One heart, one mind, and one set of eyes strong enough to make me want to wait and push away everyone else trying to fill your place. One date is the beginning of what can be.

Let's be open and free.

Believe in me.

Black is Beautiful

ALL SHADES

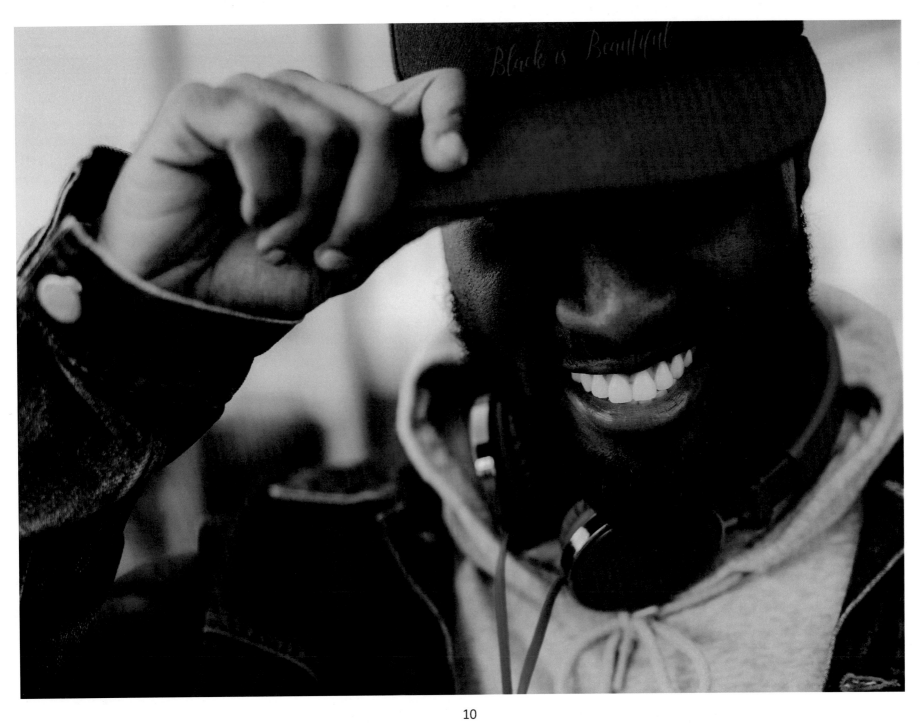

10

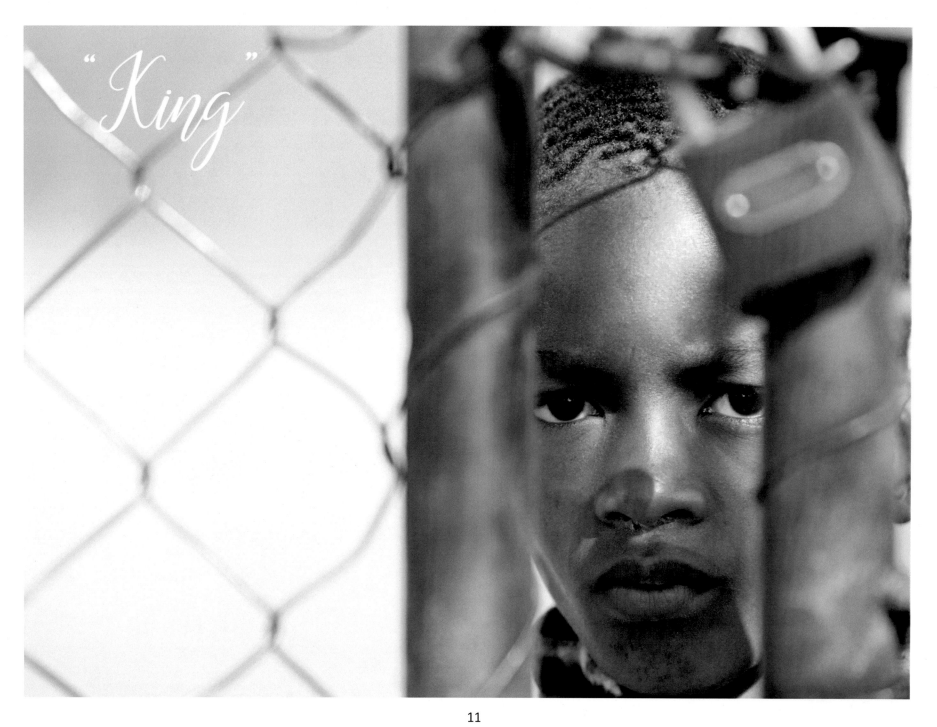

"King"

"King"

I Am a King
A great seed of excellence
A child prodigy

I will no longer wallow in the shadow of your cerebral limitations

Neglecting me

Forcing me

Chaining me

To the walls you create, then besiege

Free your mind of hate and negativity

I Am more than what you see

I Am Love

In need of love and divine protection

My Black is Diamond

My voice is Lion

My skin rich, diverse, and infused with gold

My features bold

My talents ordained by God for the world to one day know

Stay woke

Many talents will be left untold

I Am the Young Black Nation

Free your mind of discrimination

Remove the locks and chains of your mental restrictions

I Am more than what you see

I Am Love

A great and prominent seed

A golden child

I Am a King

All I need is love and meaningful navigation

Through this cold world's selective education

Massive manipulation by the radio and television stations

I will no longer wallow in the shadow of your psychosomatic boundaries

Criminalization

Negative expectations

And misguided interpretations

My souls reach is far greater than you can see

Release Me

From your gun barrels isolation and unnecessary assassinations

Free Me

Of your stereotypes and racial segregation

Your school to prison pipeline accumulation

All I need is love and a solid foundation

I Am the cornerstone of my community

I Am a King

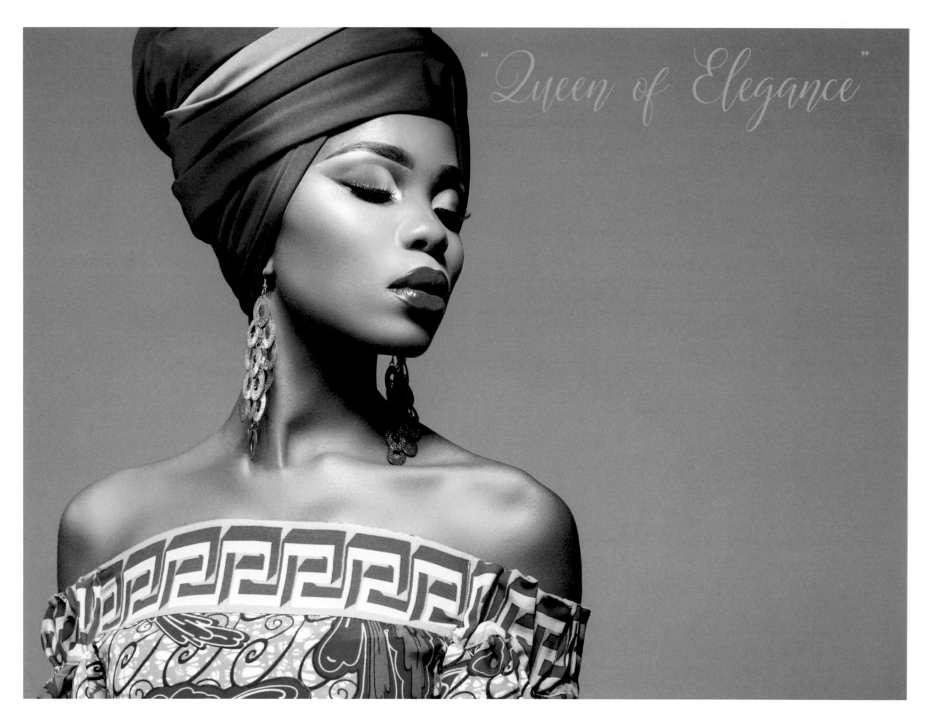

"Queen of Elegance"

15

"Queen of Elegance"

Queen of Elegance
So pure with maturity
Bursting with beauty
Sugary brown skin
Shining like gold
Sparkling with love
Your style sacred as a dove
Electrifying
Your aura is bold, lovely, and meek
The aroma radiating from your skin is sweet
Most Supreme African Fruit your beauty is distinct
Your minds capacity for knowledge reaches beyond human belief
Your focus and sense of discipline
Is astonishing to most that you meet
The depths of your heart extend beyond the deepest blue seas
Your elegant dance and soft voice are safe with me
You are the prime example of a woman
A mother
A leader
Role model and teacher
You are the prime example of everything I aspire to be
Excellence
You are within me, living and breathing within me
African Queen
Rise and step into your destiny
Be encouraged
Queen of Elegance

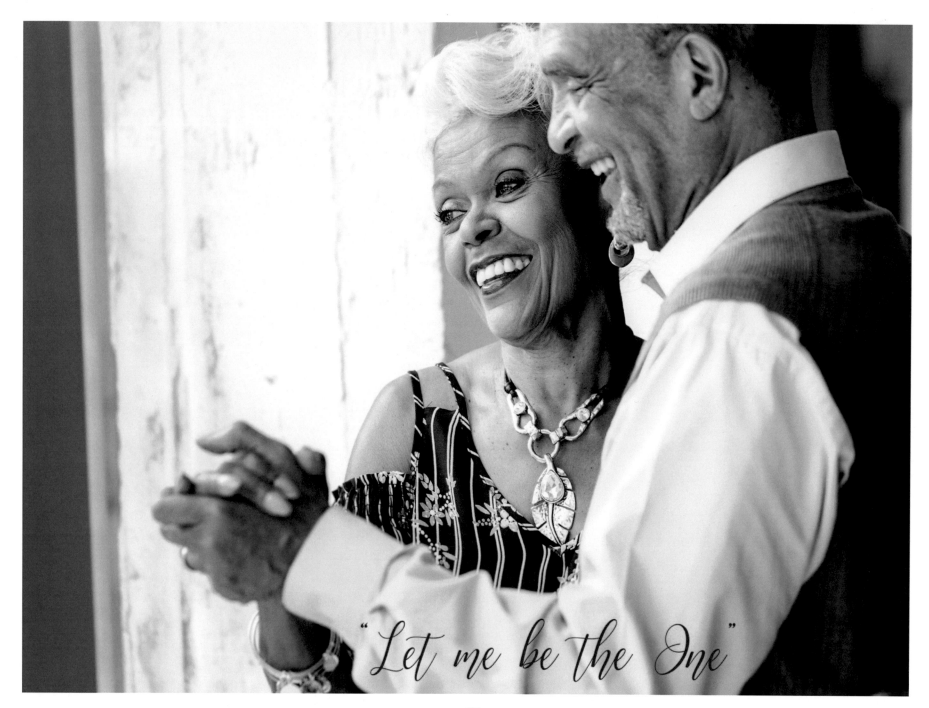

"Let me be the One"

"Let me be the One"

Let me be that soft pinch on the back of your arm
Requesting your attention
That soft voice singing through your left ear
Hoping to reach your heart
Let me be the reason for the sweat in the palm of your hands
Simply because…
Loves touch is close and anew
Let me be the one to cause your voice to crack in mid conversation
Because…
Loves presence unexpectedly crossed your path
Let me be the jitter in your bones and cold rush of energy throughout your body
To your surprise
In this moment
Loves aura has finally arrived
I want to be the one you can trust
My mind, heart, and soul will forever be loyal
I promise to be the one that loves you plentifully
Unconditionally
I will be the one to withstand the test of time
And I want to be the one that you love beyond our lifetime
Love One
Imagine me at your heart's doorstep
Knocking softly and waiting patiently
Asking you love to let me back in
Sweetheart
Let me be the one

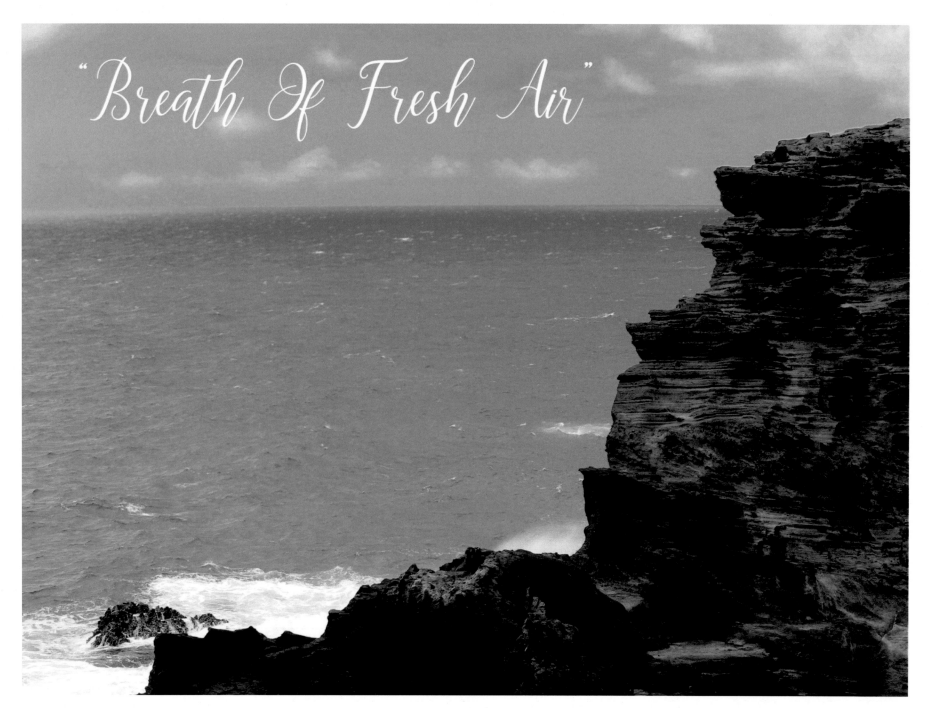

"Breath Of Fresh Air"

"Breath of Fresh Air"

You are a Breath of Fresh Air

The only sunshine in the night hour

The bluest blue flower in a garden bed

You stand out amongst many

You attract light and project the lovely colors of life

I appreciate your energy and existence

You intrigue my mind, uplift my spirit, bring joy to my eyes

And the will to strive forward to my heart

You are a Breath of Fresh Air

As I look at you from afar

I witness joy and breathe in happiness

I admire your style and daydream of your silhouette

Your peaks, curves, valleys, and summits

Gold radiance and heavenly brown tones

This journey through the abyss

Evolving and anew

I see you

Your head continuously raised high

Cheek bones grazing the sky

You are a Breath of Fresh Air

The most desired surprise

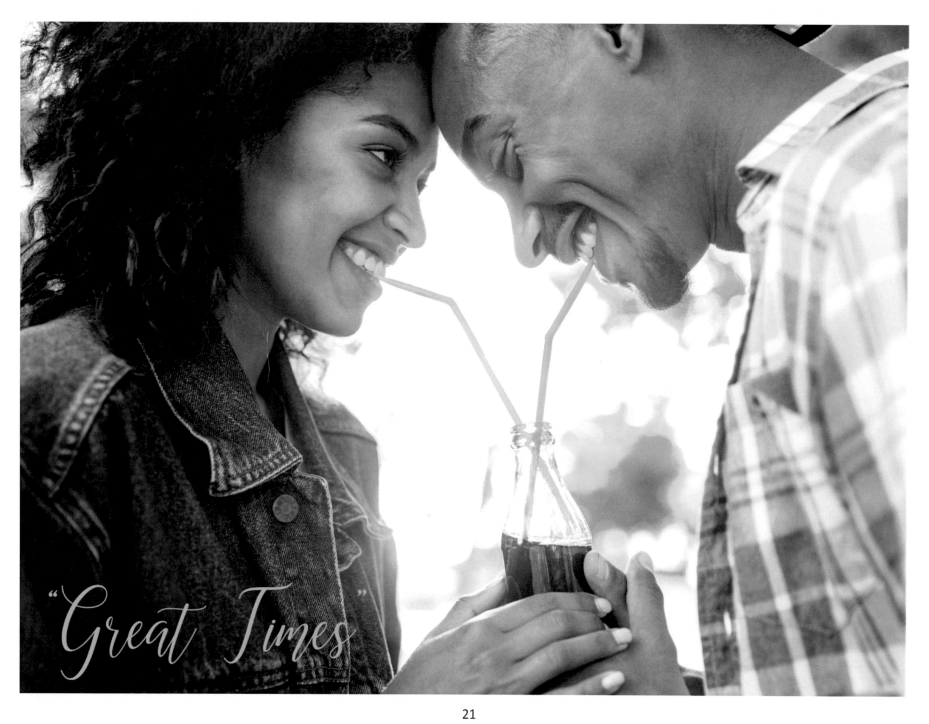

"Great Times"

"Great Times"

The great times were

Just being able to talk to you

Looking into your eyes

Witnessing your smile

Being where you are

Feeling welcomed

Spending time in your presence

Flirting with you

Spiritually conversing with you

Furthermore

Knowing that you were feeling the same way as I

Butterflies…

Those were the great times

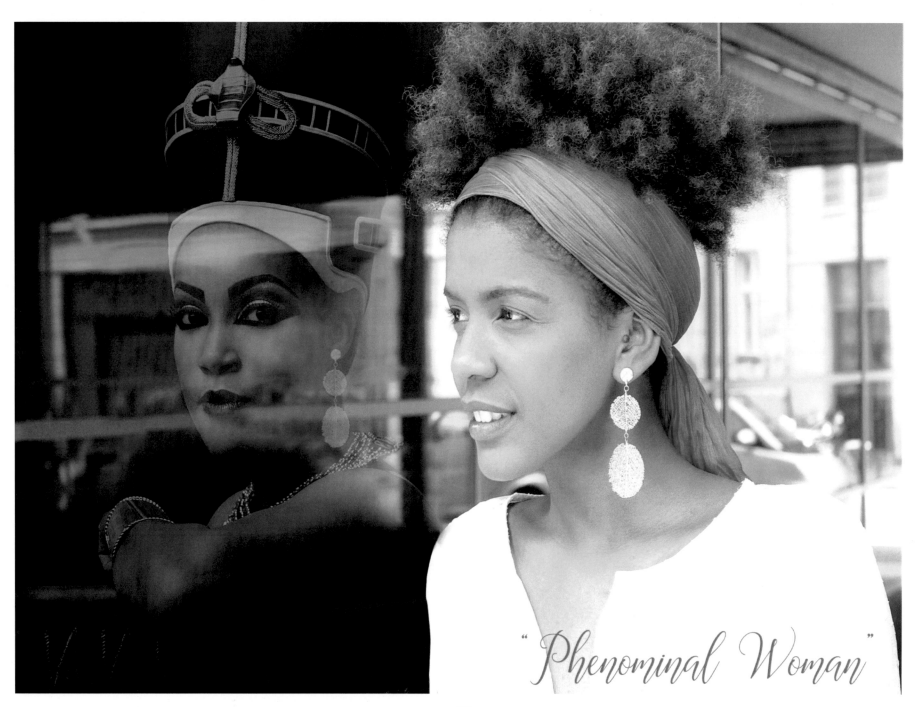

"Phenominal Woman"

"Phenomenal Woman"

Phenomenal Woman
Overflowing with positivity and exquisite beauty
Graceful, intellectual, and witty
Kindhearted, ambitious, poised, and distinct
Gorgeous, sexy, prominent, and unique
Astonishing, tantalizing, sugary, black berries, and honey hues
Thick dimensions right where they need to be
Sweet and firm
Voluptuous or petite
Best believe this Phenomenal Woman carries herself with the upmost respect and dignity
Exotic, unpredictable, educated, and humble
Self-reliant, self-assured, and gifted to teach
She is full of life
A true pleasure to meet
The complete definition of a QUEEN
Dear Phenomenal Woman
This is what I see
Reflecting back through the mirror at me…
I AM a Queen
Say it loud
Say it proud
A Phenomenal Black Woman
Yes, she is ME

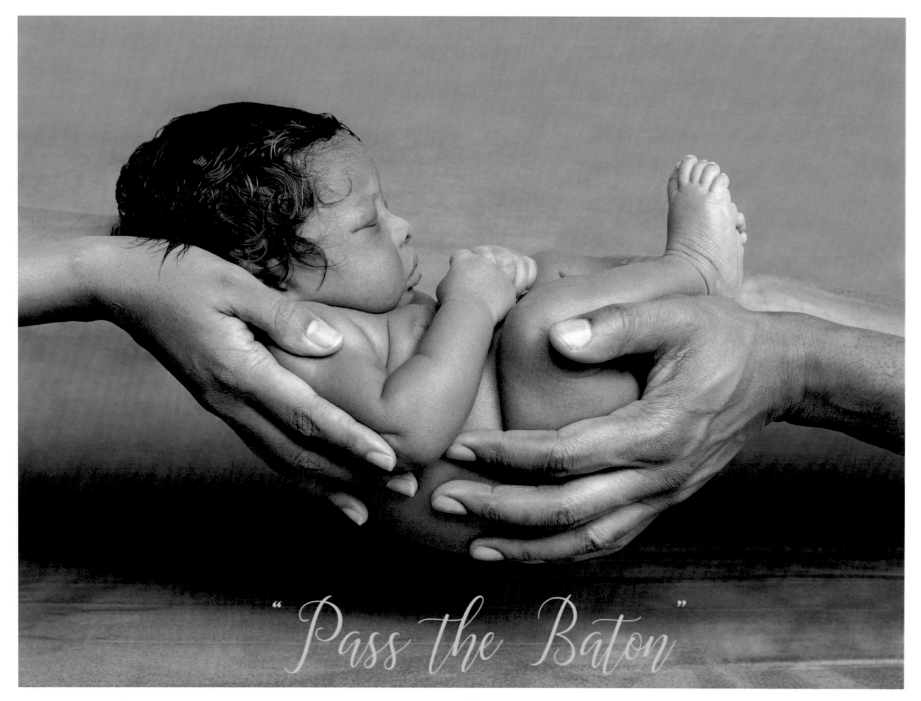

"Pass the Baton"

"Pass the Baton"

Elders, Mothers, Fathers, Teachers

Soul Inspirators, Ancestors

WE need you

To teach, educate, cultivate our roots

Pollinate, plant seeds, and enrich our hoods

Teach ME

I AM The Young Black Nation

Be my souls' compass

Continue to pass ME the Baton of strength

Pass the Baton of knowledge, morality, and inner peace

This journey has sustained centuries without ease

Do not give up

There is hope

Elders you may be tired

You may be disappointed or feel dismayed

Do not be discouraged

Do not be afraid

Or too fed up to state your case

Teach ME

The Young Black Nation

Keep Passing the Baton of self- love and honor

Speak your truth

Until it penetrates

And breaks the yoke that produces change

The Young Black Nation needs you

Lead ME

With your wisdom

Lead ME

With the truth of your experience

Tell ME the truth of our people

WE are Kings and Queens

Gifted inventors and possessors of skillful trades

WE are trend setters, leaders, and entrepreneurs'

Elders

I AM The Young Black Nation

I need to hear your words in order to see

If your words are unwelcomed or ignored

Still speak

Pass the Baton of respect and unity

This Young Black Nation needs serenity

Distinguished Leaders

Preach

I need to absorb the infinite knowledge of our Black History

Don't leave me alone to figure it out on my own

WE need Front-Runners and

Elders who refuse to give up on ME and my generation

Remind ME of the code of conduct

To show respect towards my elders

Respecting my own and sticking together

Teach ME through demonstration

I know WE can be rude and unruly at times

Ungrateful and even take your wisdom for granted

Elders please forgive ME

I AM the Young Black Nation

Continue to shed light

Don't throw in the towel

Don't throw your hands up and dismiss ME

Teach ME in the mist of this spiritual rivalry

War between green and seasoned

Juvenile and Astute

Black on Black

Man, versus Machine

Show US what it takes to be considered Kings and Queens

WE need your stories of conquer and defeat

Struggle and pain

Trials and triumphs

Show ME what I should aspire to be

So that I can pass gems of authenticity along to those subsequently

I am asking you Black Excellence

Pleading with your wisdom and maturity to continue to teach

Your knowledge and experience are key

Share with ME

Even if you think it's just passing through ME

Like the howl of the winds from a speeding train

Unconsciously

I AM listening

Pivotal points in life give rise to your words spoken over ME

Don't be disheartened

Even if I temporarily lose my mind

Smack my lips

Talk back

Give you attitude

Roll my head and my eyes

Then out of pride

Tell you that "I don't care"

Believe ME Elders

I AM listening

With the grace of Almighty GOD

Please be patient with ME

Mold ME

Continue to scold ME

Put ME in my place

While you hold ME

Close to your heart

If I drop the Baton and drop all the clues

Repeatedly

Pray over ME and…

Tell ME what YOU would do

Tell ME to pick myself up

And get it together

Hold my head up high

And never wither

My head may be thick

And my ass may be soft but...

Elders keep Passing the Baton

Your experience holds the atlas to life

Your wisdom is the pathway to enlightenment

Unknowingly

Your voice sits with ME

In the silence

Replaying your words of wisdom over again continuously

In this world of lies

Manipulation and deception

Electronics, fake friends, and social antics…

The touch of my love ones and true connection is weak

Almost obsolete

Give ME proof

Which, manifests through your truth

Keep it real with ME

I am on the road of life discovering who I will be

Elders keep Passing the Baton

WE need you…

Sincerely

The Young Black Nation

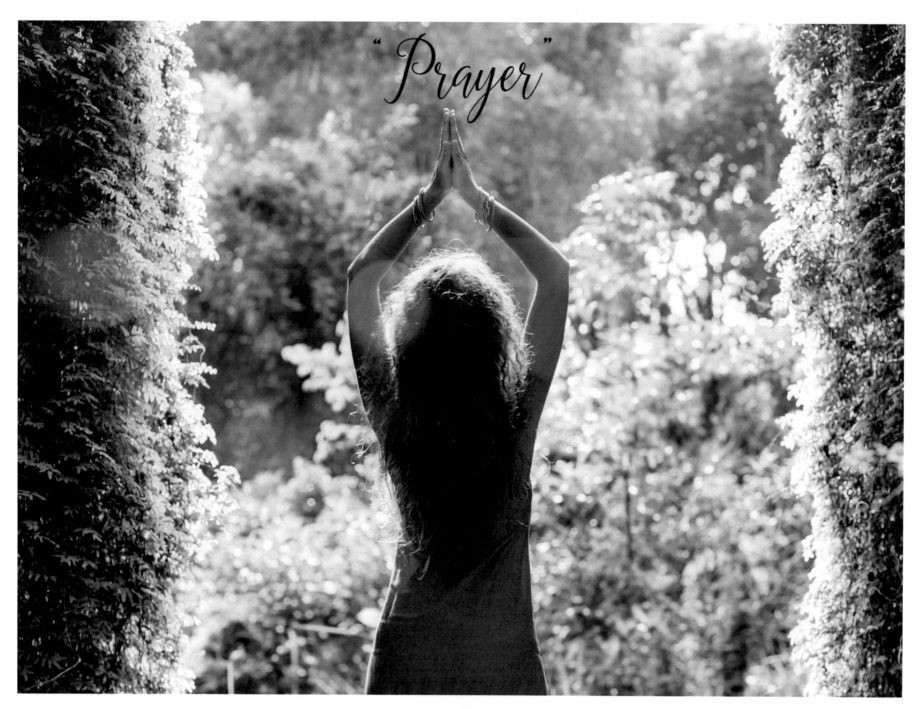

"Prayer"

I prayed for the confidence to approach you

When you extended your hand

I accepted

My soul fell into place

My puzzle was complete

Sweat perspiring from both of our hands

I allowed space in between

Just to let our hands

Breathe

Shortly after my inexperience

Caused you to walk away

Now

I wish I had held on tighter

And prayed

For the patience and confidence

To listen to, believe in and follow my own spirit

Forgive me Lord

I should have said thanks

And prayed

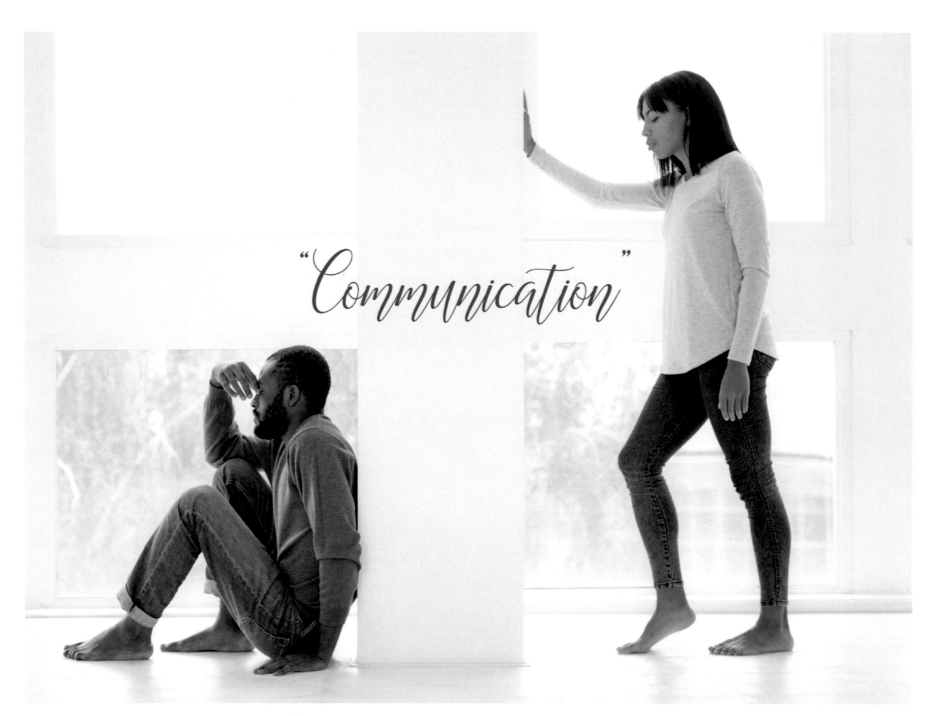

"Communication"

"Communication"

Talk to me
Communicate openly
No boundaries
No walls
Trust me
Forgive me
Mutual respect and solidarity
Let us build
A two-way street labeled
Equal Exchange
Lovie
Without communication
We leave room for infiltration
Miscommunication
Misunderstandings
Conflict and confusion
Anxiety and overthinking
My emotions and decision making sway unsteadily on the balance beam
Due to the fear of you leaving me
That energy has stolen so many years
I am sorry
Without communication
We will only share
Lost opportunities
Heartbreak & Separation
Lovie
I am afraid
Please open up and talk to me

"Silence"

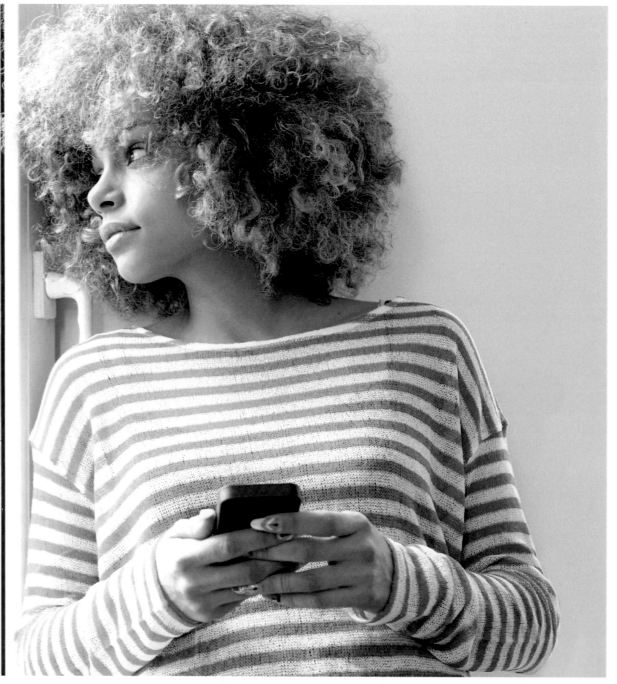

"Silence"

The silence

Is calling me

The silence is calling for me to follow my heart

Loudly

Profoundly

On the other hand

My eyes are telling my mind another

My eyes

Only see you ignoring me

Avoiding me

Acting like you don't even know me

My eyes

Only see you not around

Then again

In the silence

A soft calming voice says from within

Listen to your heart

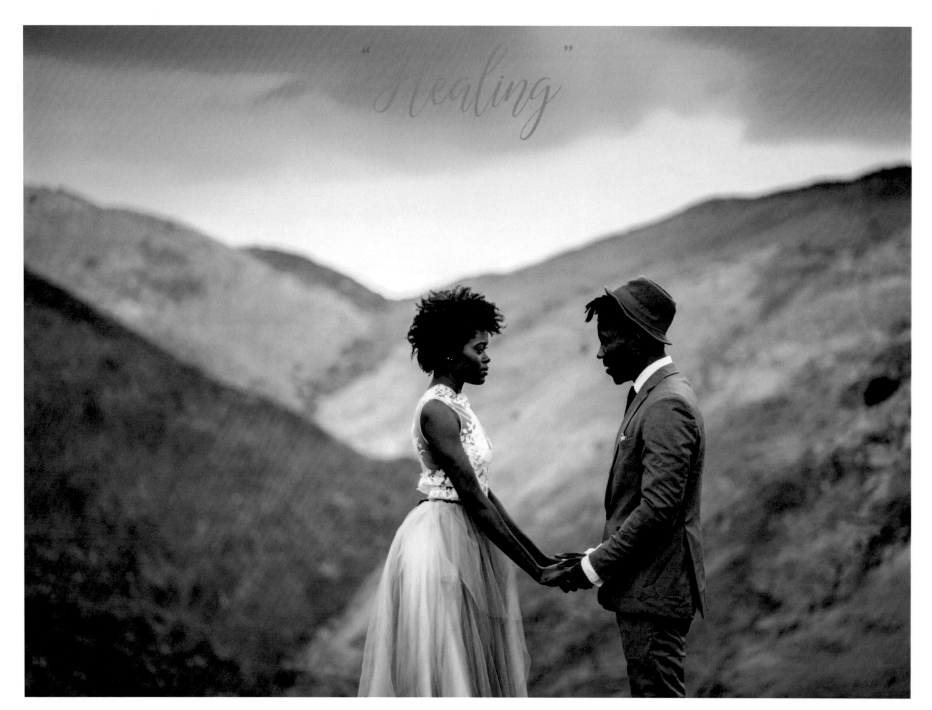

"Healing"

If time can heal...

Can respect build trust?

-Monique L. DeSargant

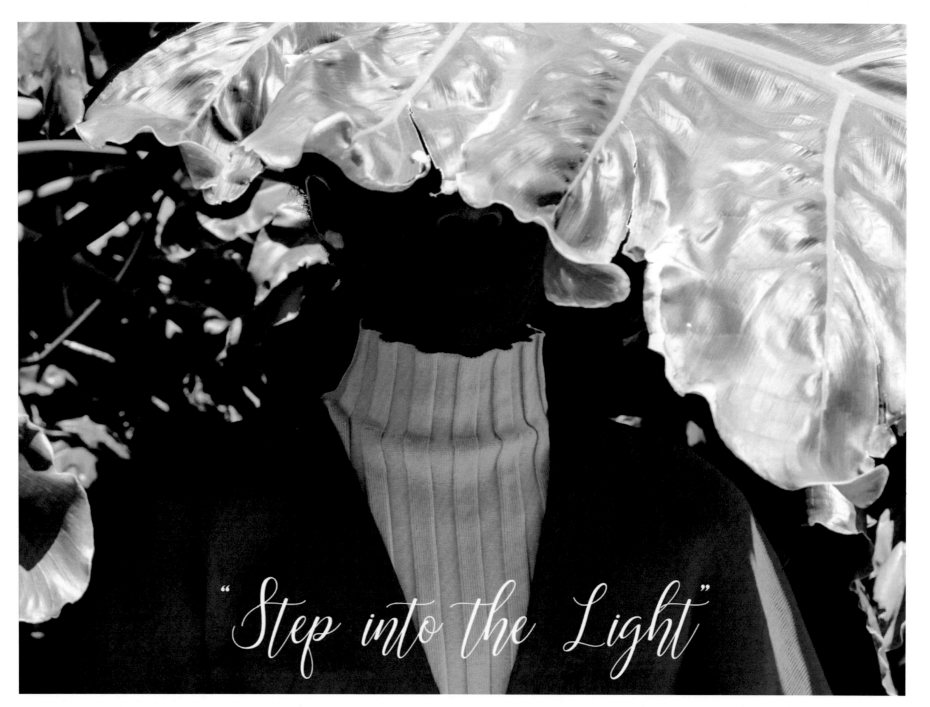

"Step into the Light"

"Step into the Light"

Under the shadows of disappointment and despair
Your heart chakra maybe in need of repair
You have asked
You have prayed
You have envisioned
Loves presence everywhere
Now breath
Believe
And listen
Step into the Light
Be bold
Take risks
Lift your head
Black Nation
Then step into your next dimension
Bask in the joy and richness of the sun
Rise higher
Your melanated bloodline is essential
Move forward my Love
Beyond the shadows
You deserve love, loyalty, and laughter
Healing, positive energy and new beginnings
Let your soul be your guide
"I AM HERE," says Love
Step into the Light

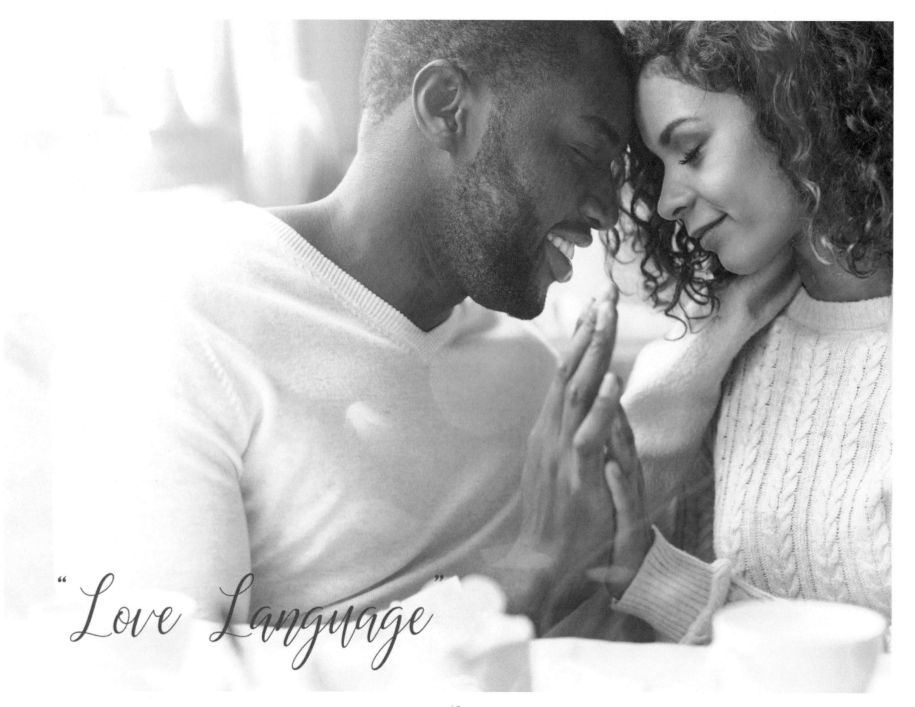

"Love Language"

"Love Language"

We embody
A spiritual language of love
A love translated through energy and connection
The most passionate language of them all

You hear me
Speaking without words
A love unseen
A hidden frequency

Conversing without verbal exchange
You reply
Talking with only our eyes
From across the crowd
Only we know the dialogue that is shared
Sensation without touch
Energy conveyed through space and time
An essence with the power of tsunami winds
Resonating solely between you and I

Butterflies arise

When our eyes unite

A private intimacy

Stimulating mental affections

For filling the empty space

Electricity taps my shoulder

Whenever you enter a room

Or when your presence is near

I sense you

Love unspoken

And it was love before I knew your name

Emotions taken higher with every encounter

Feeling you close even though you are far away

Unwanted space

Provoking the heart to create

A love unknown and unheard of to ordinary men

In the flesh

We are practically strangers

In the spirit

We have developed a relationship

Deeper than most have imagined

Or could even comprehend

It's too deep to be explained

However, the sensation is eagerly seeked

And its foundation and creation

Are heavily craved to be understood

Across Nations

Border Lines

Cultures and time

While at rest

It's your spirit that pays the occasional visit

Leaving behind blessings in the form of hope

Wisdom, insight, and words of encouragement

You have mastered the art of subliminal messaging

Capturing and challenging the mind

Your style is one of a kind

Lovie, you are number one in my heart

Keeping your best interest in mind is priority

Protecting your name, image and spirit has always held validity

From afar, I sense the love of a lifetime

Within my heart you feel like the love of my life

Those that I've experienced in the physical

Don't compare to you

Your very existence moves me

And your spiritual signature

Has left its eternal inscription within me

Love at first sight

If I had to define it

It would begin with you

And describe every moment we have shared since the very start

Love One, you still have my heart

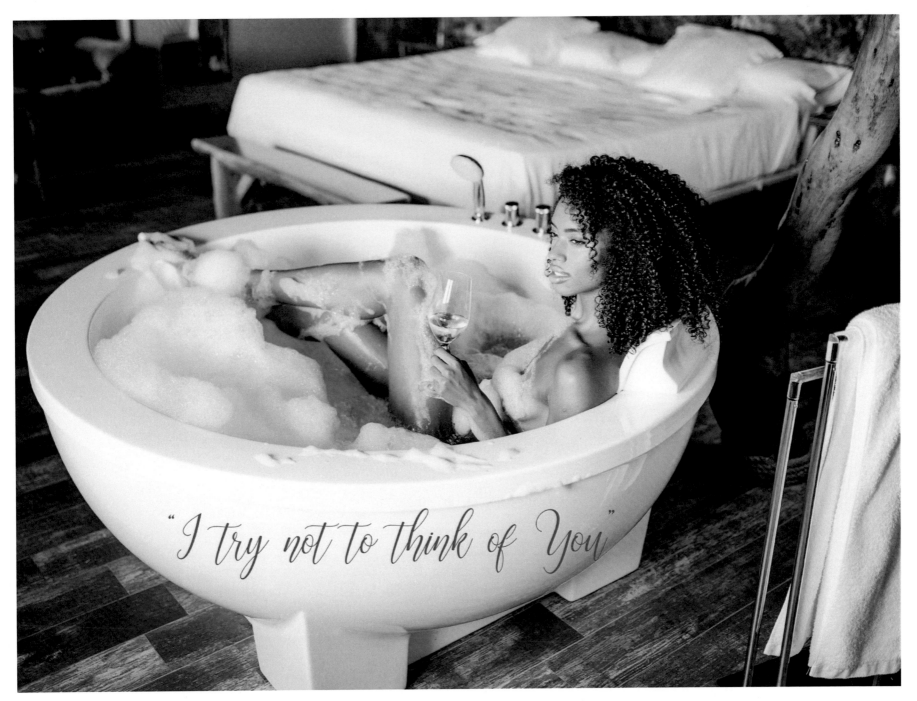

"I try not to think of you"

I try not to think of you

I try not to picture your lovely smile or your eyes burning in mine

I try not to laugh at the thoughts and beautiful memories you have given me

I try not to remember your hand reaching out for mine

Inviting me

Enticing me

I try not to remember the song I sung in your direction

Through your left ear and into your heart

I try not to remember the butterflies tickling at my heart

My intestines turning Double Dutch within my belly whenever you enter a room

I try not to remember all the first times you have given me

Like loving you at first sight, feeling nervous, scared, and unprepared

Dropping the glass before the taste could even touch my lips

Scrambling to pick up and glue the pieces

Tears, Anita Baker songs, choosing to spend nights alone

Waking up many nights at the crack of dawn because my heart was torn

I still hope you won't be gone for long

Reality is you make my soul smile, my feet tap

My hands sweat and my heart do the James Brown

I can't fight it

Your essence is a TKO

I want to be in your corner, on your team, in all your classes and everywhere else in between

Sometimes, the thought of you takes me to a place of sensuality

Although my respect for you is high

I try not to imagine you kissing me

Touching me

Inside of me

All over me

And we pleasing we

You make me so excited

But I try not to think about it

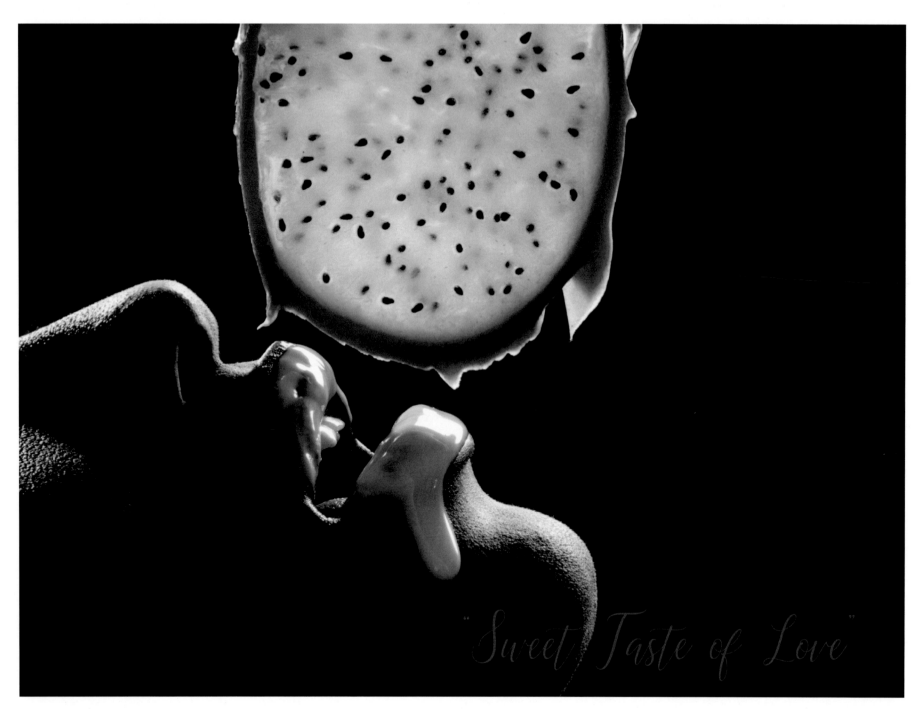

"Sweet Taste of Love"

"Sweet Taste of Love"

Exotic sweet succulents and harvested fruits like watermelon, mango, pineapple, black plums, and honeydew, I enjoy tremendously. However, my taste buds desire to indulge in your flavor. Could it be warm, soft, and sweet like half sliced peaches with cream? Maybe it's wet and sugary, like strawberries diced and marinated in sweet juices of sugar cane? Or could it simply be addicting like tearing thick red juicy grapes away from their vine? The essence of your passion fruit feels so close, intense and exhilarates my soul. My lips have only pondered the taste of your flavor; however, I know those sweet and sour Tamarinds immersed in brown sugar molasses are well worth the wait. The fragrance of your fresh fruit is stimulating like the sensation of an aphrodisiac. Push those Anjou pears in my mouth and listen to me smack. There is no need for napkins sweetie, I like it when it's wet, messy, running down my chin, and the back of my hands. I won't let your tropical love go to waste. So, I promise not to miss a spot, and I intend on consuming every drop. My metabolism is high, so indulging multiple times in your Dragon fruit would be the treat of a lifetime. African Miracle fruit and berries, your cultivation nurtures and arouses pleasant emotions.

Can I taste you?

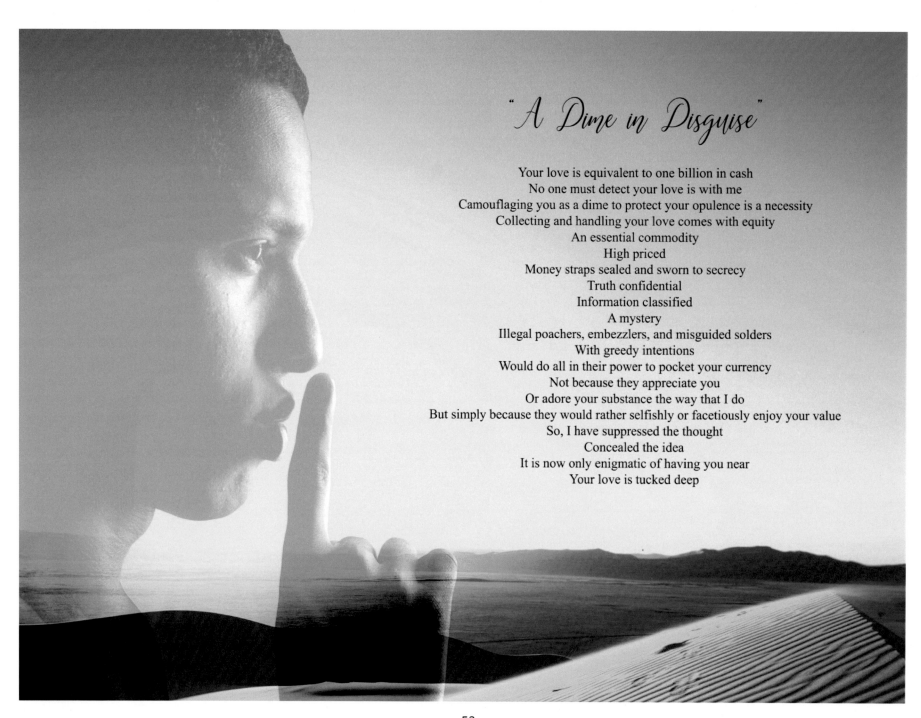

"A Dime in Disguise"

Your love is equivalent to one billion in cash
No one must detect your love is with me
Camouflaging you as a dime to protect your opulence is a necessity
Collecting and handling your love comes with equity
An essential commodity
High priced
Money straps sealed and sworn to secrecy
Truth confidential
Information classified
A mystery
Illegal poachers, embezzlers, and misguided solders
With greedy intentions
Would do all in their power to pocket your currency
Not because they appreciate you
Or adore your substance the way that I do
But simply because they would rather selfishly or facetiously enjoy your value
So, I have suppressed the thought
Concealed the idea
It is now only enigmatic of having you near
Your love is tucked deep

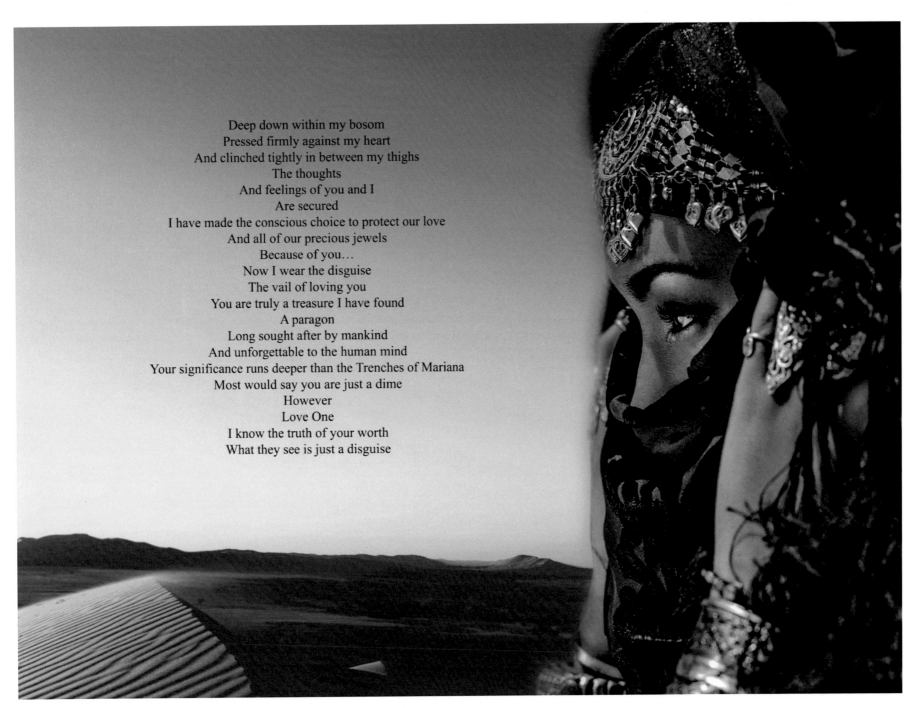

Deep down within my bosom
Pressed firmly against my heart
And clinched tightly in between my thighs
The thoughts
And feelings of you and I
Are secured
I have made the conscious choice to protect our love
And all of our precious jewels
Because of you…
Now I wear the disguise
The vail of loving you
You are truly a treasure I have found
A paragon
Long sought after by mankind
And unforgettable to the human mind
Your significance runs deeper than the Trenches of Mariana
Most would say you are just a dime
However
Love One
I know the truth of your worth
What they see is just a disguise

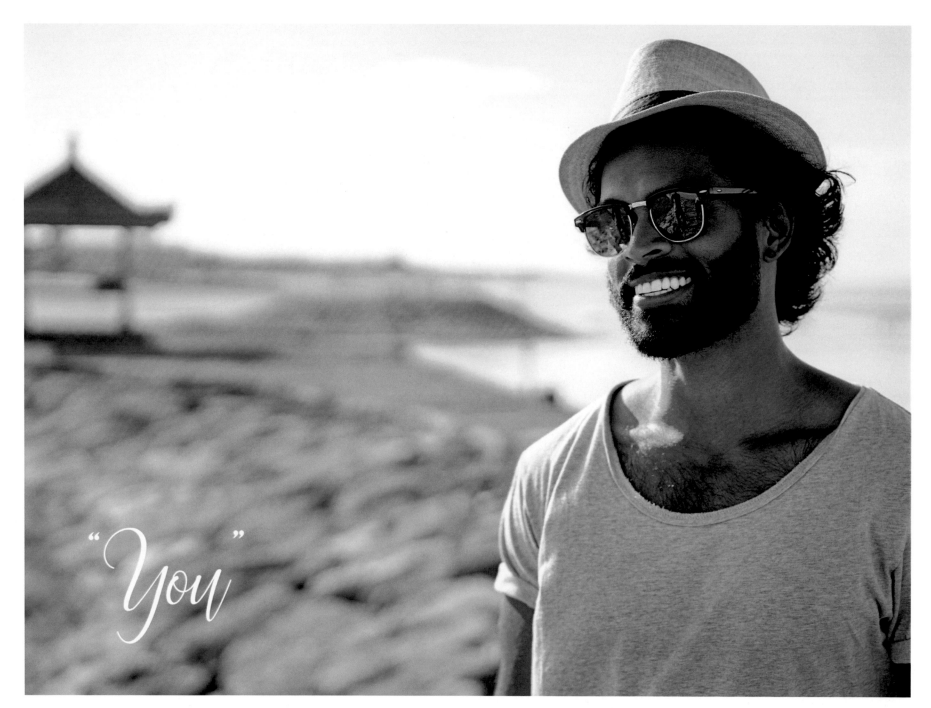

"You"

"You"

Looking at you

Is like seeing a diamond

For the very first time

No smiles just yet

Only staring beauty in the eye

My mind screaming

"DAMN, you fine"

When the sparkle of your smile

Hits my eyes

My heart and soul

Begin to shine

You project all the beautiful colors of the rainbow

Your formula is pure

A precious stone

Created to cure all broken hearts and wounds

You are the sparkle of my eye

And the memories I wish to dream

Diamonds are a girl's best friend

And you…

I have already placed in my heart

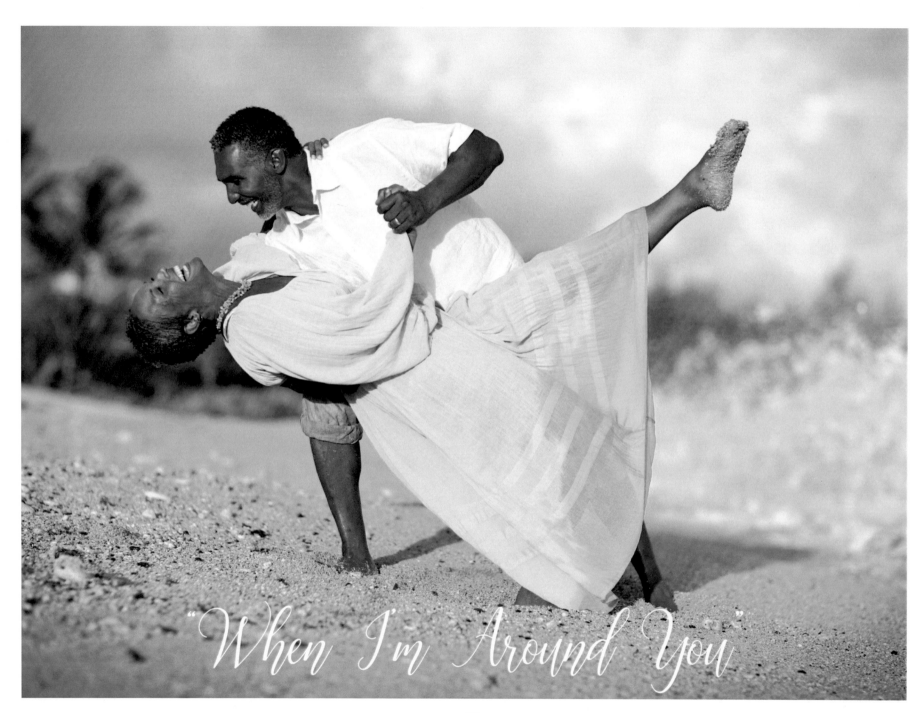

"When I'm Around You"

"When I'm Around You"

When I'm around you
I feel a mystical energy pulsating through my veins
Joy overflows
You are graceful
Like the sand pouring through an hourglass
I can feel each and every grain
You make me softer inside
Permeable outside
More willing to listen to and absorb the wisdom that radiates from your center
Your light illuminates like the omnipresent moon
Your presence awakens my soul
I am proud to know you
Honored to grow with you
Love one
Your role in my life is notable
I am grateful
Our souls have connected on the highest plateau
Under God and indivisible
When I'm around you
My soul is continually ballooned
Your presence is worth more than gold
I love being around you

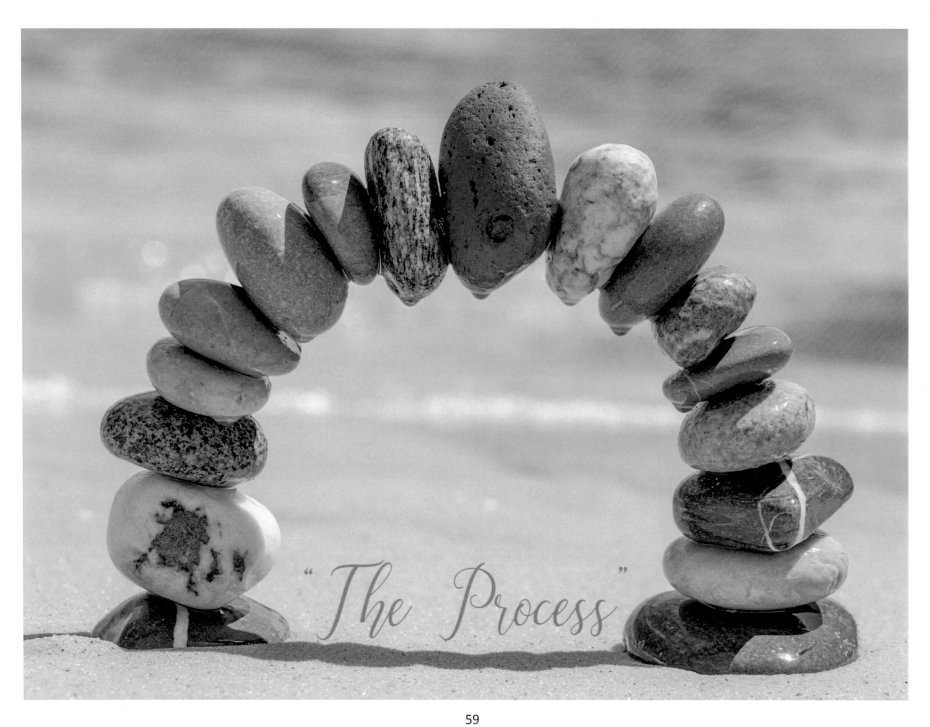

"The Process"

"The Process"

Trust is a process

Built through a series of actions

Which takes time

Respect

Peace

Love

Patience

Then…

Serenity

Trust the process

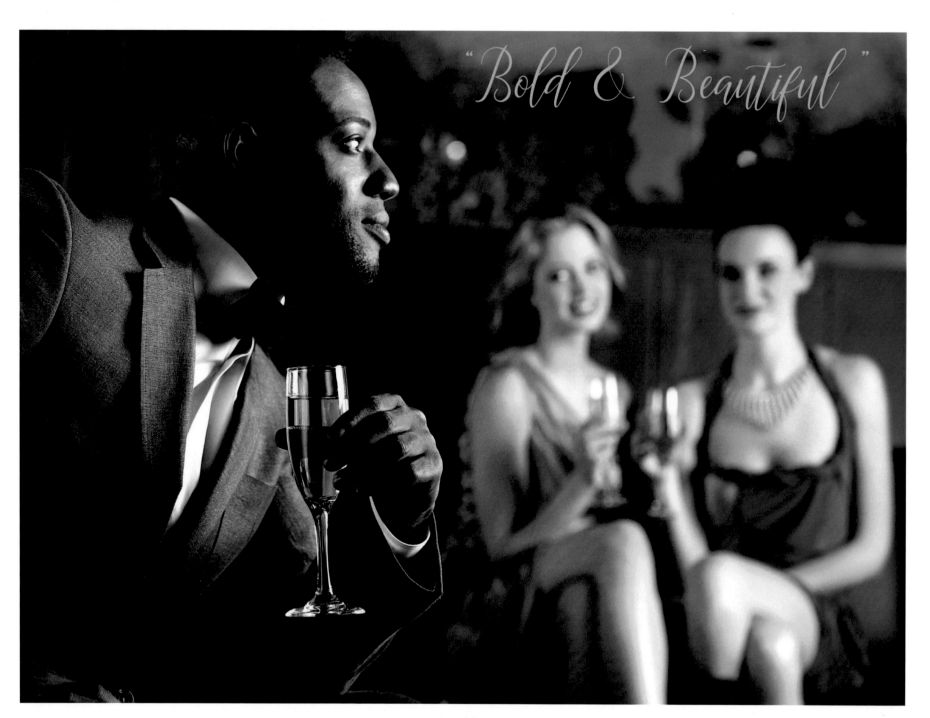

"Bold & Beautiful"

"*Bold & Beautiful*"

Who is that?

With all that jazz

Impeccable smile and upbeat style

Who is He?

That intrigues and triggers all my senses

And fills my mind and soul with glee

That man...

Bold and Beautiful Black man

Bursting with confidence and pizazz

Sophistication and swag

That fine Brotha over there…

Commanding all of my attention

From a distance

I am compelled

His mental persuasion and visual persistence

Is seductive

Got me like DAMN!!

Who gave him all that bass and cello?

My eyes and lips are stuck

Fixated

While my heart giggles HELLO!!

His presence gives me life

His scent is tantalizing

Got me fantasizing and visualizing of

Running my fingers up and down

All 88 keys of his Big Black Grand Piano

The impeccable structure of a Black King

Brimming over with strength and panache

A steel-clad

Laced with gold and industrial metals

Bold, Black and Beautiful

A classic

This Black man is

Art Deco

A phenomenon

In his own right

Black Renaissance

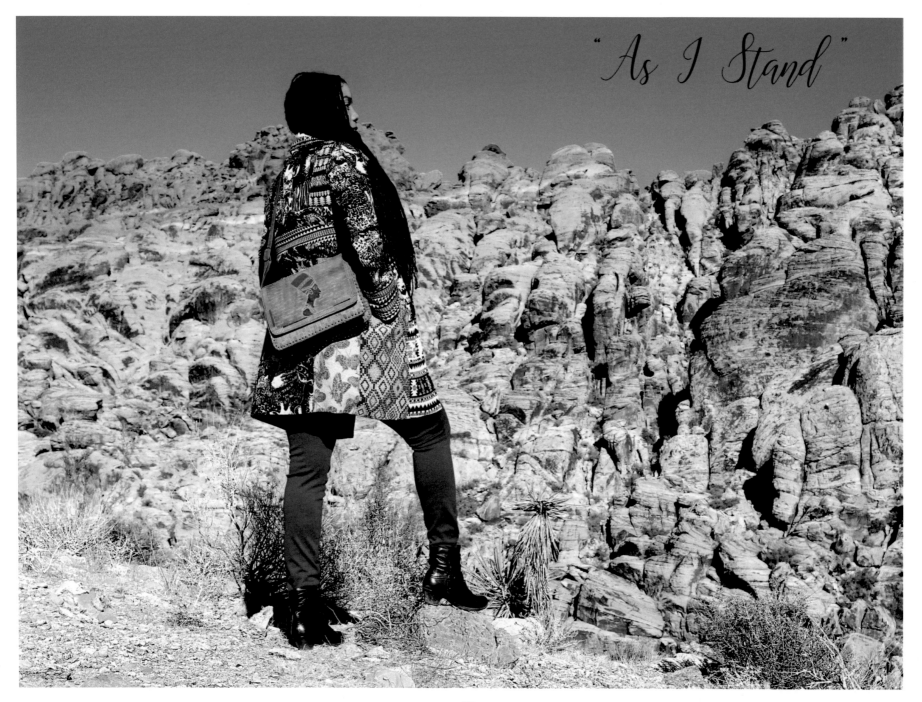

"As I Stand"

"As I Stand"

As I stand
Here on this rock of faith
Holding my shoulder bag of patience
My hair locked and filled with our memories

I wait
For the one I have only known as Love
Love has taken me to the highest cloud
And sent me back down
Crashing through the marine
To face the bottom of the sea
Only my belief in God
Along with his favor, grace and mercy brought me out

Regardless of all
Come rain or shine
The thought of your Love still fills me with joy
You are the only one I long for
And the only one I write poetic hymns about
You hold the keys to my heart

Love One
Re-open the chambers you closed long ago
And re-enter the valves

For which only your name is engraved
Once in a lifetime we may find a friendship worth waiting for
Still
My heart and mind both equally ajar
And beating rhythmically in your hands
Love, you asked me to, "wait."
In all honesty
Achieving the blessing of having you near is well worth the delay

So, I stand
Here on this rock of faith
Holding my shoulder bag of patience
My hair locked and filled with our memories

I wait
For the one whose movement resembles the fluttering of a butterfly
Your aura sweeter than my grandma's sweet potato pie
When you speak
Romance is in your voice
And the taste of caramel I imagine upon your lips
You light up the sky with merely your presence and style
Your skin tone shimmering honey brown
You behold the most beautiful pair of eyes and charming smile

The joyful bounce in your walk
Is captivating
My eyes hit the jack pot each and every time
My mind humbly filled with admiration and curiosity
You are distinct in every way

Breathtaking like the first glance of a Golden Palomino

Truth is
I have found a friendship worth waiting for
Although long and oftentimes hard
Love One
I will wait
For the day that you return
I will wait
For your eyes to once again rest in mine
And I will wait
For your hand to once again… reach out… for mine

Therefore, Love
As I stand
Here on this rock of faith
Holding my shoulder bag of patience
My hair locked and filled with our memories
Willingly
I stand

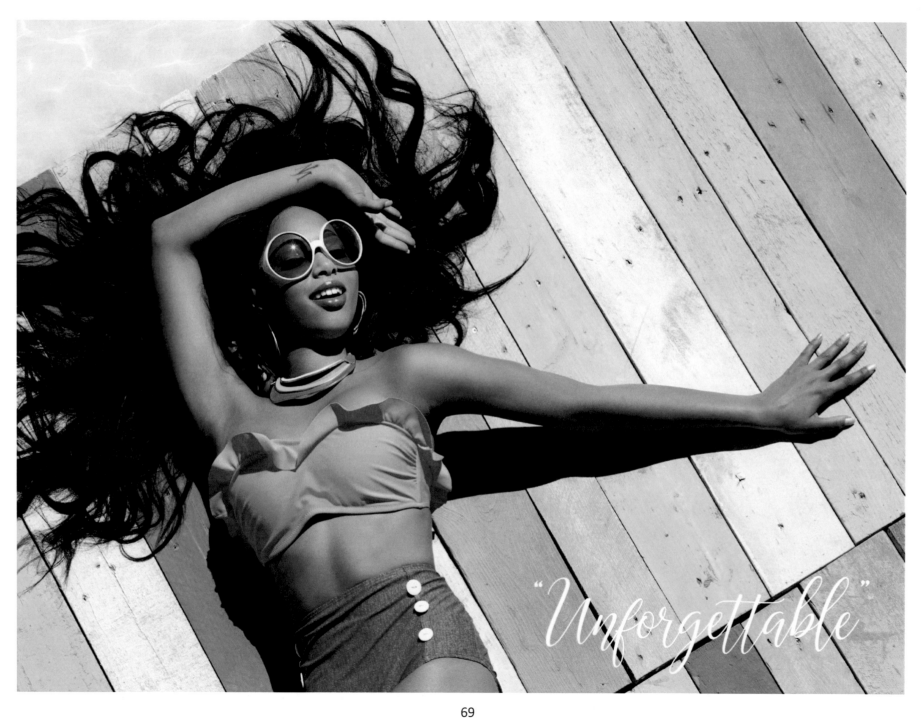

"Unforgettable"

69

"Unforgettable"

You exemplify a lovely sanctuary of gold, rubies, and pearls
Precious, impressive, and sweet as spring plums
The mere thought of your voice and smile
Formulates butterflies in my belly
You are exquisite, glowing, and shimmering with the sparkle of dancing lights
In the day and night hour
Your spirit extraordinarily shines
Projecting a positive light
Fluorescent
Iridescent
You symbolize the light that glistens in my eye
For days at a time
The image of you will not leave my mind
Your vibe mystical yet tangible
Your creative style leaves me speechless and only able to stare
However
I am boiling with conversation
Can you feel me talking?
I am eagerly wishing to share my desires
You take me higher
Come near
Come closer
Let me share your sanctuary
You are unforgettable

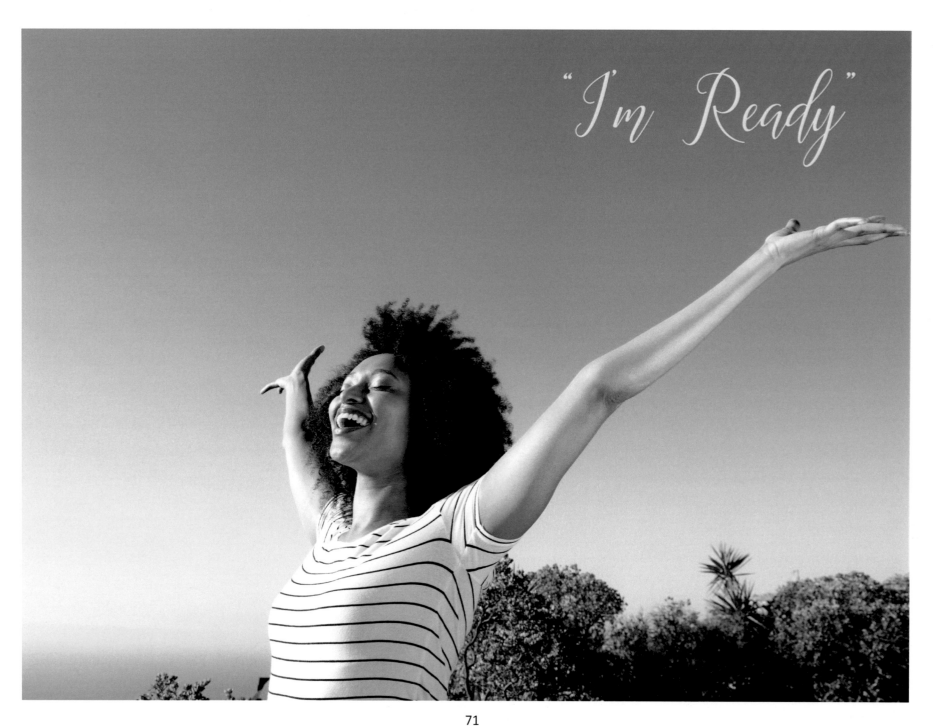

"I'm Ready"

"I'm Ready"

Love
I am no longer afraid
I am no longer running away
I am no longer intimidated
By the energy your spirit conveys

Fear, is now a thing of the past
Your liveliness is beautiful
And no longer too much for me to bare

I'm stronger now
Much wiser now
I'm ready
Hello World…
I am ready for love

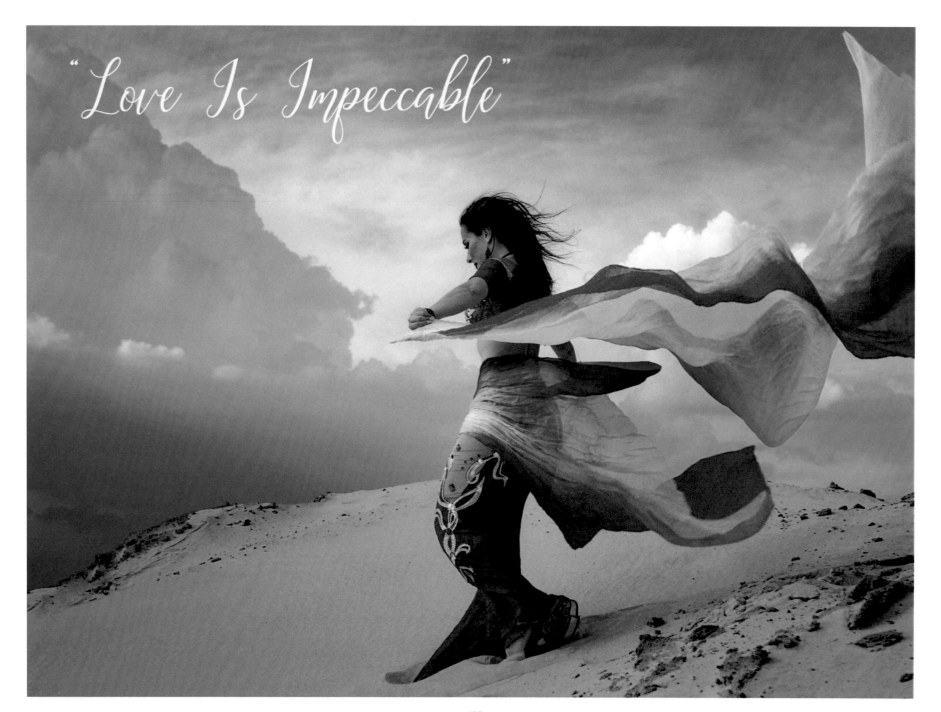

"Love Is Impeccable"

"Love is Impeccable"

Love is patient
Love is kind
Real Love is humble
Forgiving
Understanding
Genuinely connected
And equally ajar
Love is free
Love takes risks and admits truth when wrong
Loves respects space and boundaries even though it may be hard
Love will accept no when the soul hopes to hear yes
Love is incredible
Not perfect
We have all failed a test
Love what makes you happy
Sometimes love hurts
Unconditional love is unyielding an eternal mood
Deep beneath the surface
A strong current flows throughout the visible purview
Pure love endures
Demonstrates consistency and respect
Love sees no color, gender, social or economic status
Love outside the box
And teach each other how to grow
Collectively

Without conditions, stipulations, or predetermined expectations
Spiritual connections are meant, but do not come with a directory or blueprint
Energy transforms and transcends space and time
Manifested earthly within its divine time
Give it and receive it
Freely and gratefully
Seeds of love planted securely in Mother Nature's fertile nursery
Watered and groomed by the heavenly sun
Is God's kind of Love
The entire world is in need of some
Positive possibilities are birthed and rebirthed
Time and time again
An undeniable sensation connecting spirit to man
If you look beyond your boundaries and mental limitations
You will realize Love inspires and can heal the entire nation
Seated beside Love and God
I believe there is nothing Higher
God is Love and his grace is on fire
Love is Impeccable
Take me higher

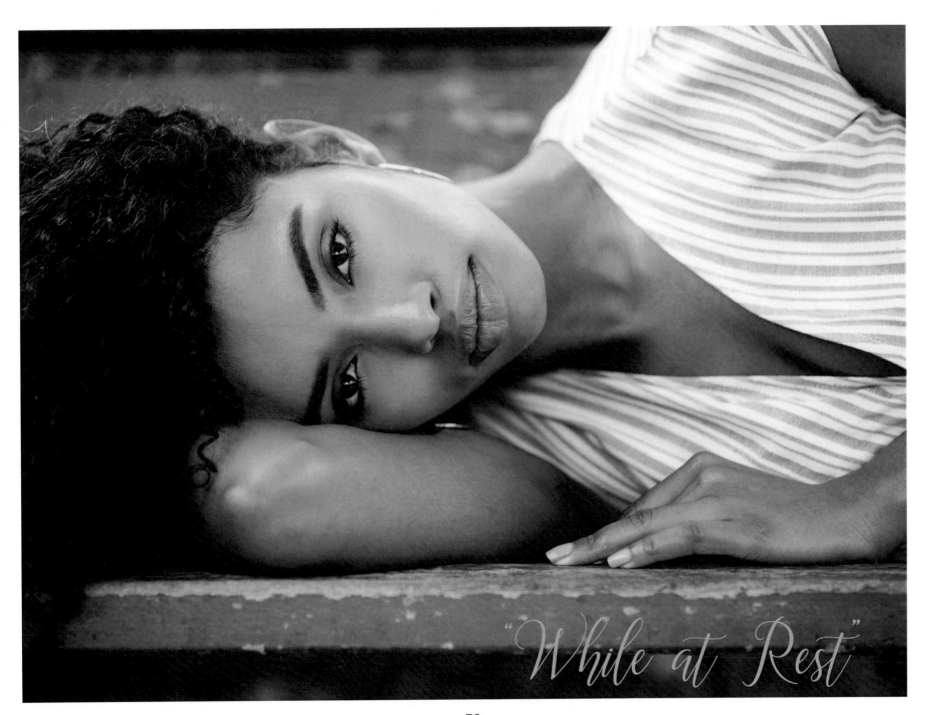

"While at Rest"

"While at Rest"

While at rest

I vividly dream…

The mist of spirituality frequently intervenes

Questions by day

Answers by night

While at rest God speaks in

Bold whispers throughout the night

Occasionally

I dream of you and me

Where you lay is where I really want to be

While awake

I must wait patiently

For the unraveling to this mystery

Our story slowly evolves overtime

With each sunrise and sunset

The pages turn and fold

The book opened and closed

Followed by shelving and dust covered jackets

Thoughts of giving up or hanging on began to overload

When dreams tarry

The mind ponders

But when love is real the heart will never wonder

I pray for guidance and strength to hold on

And rebuke the spirit of fear that infected my happy home

Revise the blueprint and press on

By day I walk in faith

At night I pray

That I will stop wasting time by making the same mistakes

I imagine you here and call love in

Dreams are more than just a beautiful representation of a magnificent imagination

Dreams provide guidance and revision

Lord please prepare me

For the arrival of loves next destination

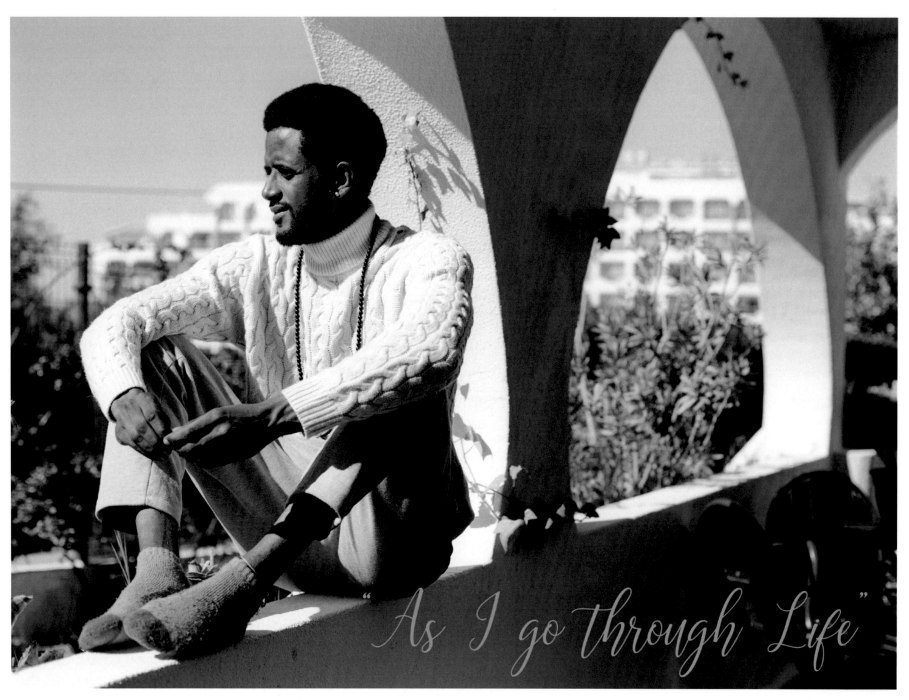

"As I go through Life"

"As I Go Through Life"

As I go through life

I think of you

When I awake each morning

I thank God

Then, I think of you

When I arrive to work

And began the assignment at hand

I think of you

Hoping that one day God will cleverly reveal

The secret of getting closer to you

When I travel locally or abroad

I sing along with every tune that reminds me of you

When I am alone

It is thoughts of you that entertain me in the silence

I carry you with me every step that I take

God makes no mistakes

You are always in my heart

As I searched for my first home

I thought of you

Now that I am a first-generation homeowner

I frequently imagine you here

As I chose the decor of my home

I kept you in mind

Shades of blue are intertwined

When I fall asleep at night

You are always in my prayers

Hoping that one day you will reappear

As I go through life

One day at a time

Love One

I still think of you

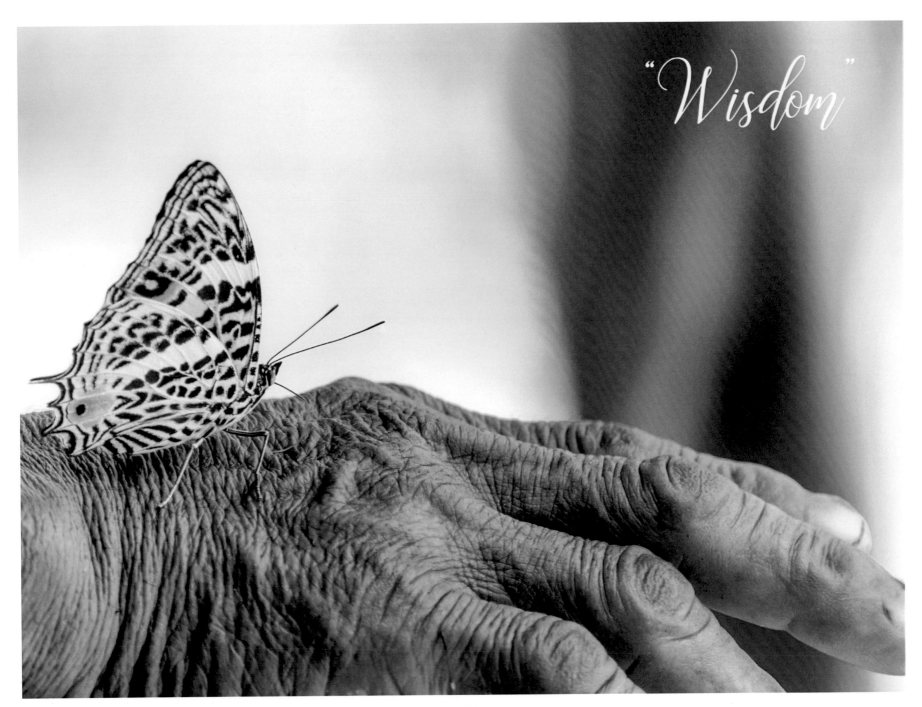

"*Wisdom*"

"Wisdom"

The act of being still

And just listening is truly a gift

A distinctive characteristic that can only be nurtured overtime

Your wisdom

Stands out in my mind

I have always admired this about you and

This is just one reason why you shine

I am consistently learning with you

Throughout time

And through each experience shared

I have gained precious jewels

Divine knowledge

Amidst the highs and lows

I have been tested

Strengthened and groomed

I have grown to know that

Quality listening is truly a work of art

Listening in the spirit

Listening through observation

Listening to body language

Listening to nature

Listening to the unexpected

Listening to the silence

Listening to my heart

And listening to the voice of God

LISTENING...

SPEAKS...

Various languages

Thank you

For allowing me to express myself

I have meant every word

I appreciate you

Your time, patience, and efforts

Your wisdom and discipline have touched my soul

In ways you may never know

My heart remains fond of you

My love for you is an open door

Be blessed Love

You are my Distant Mentor

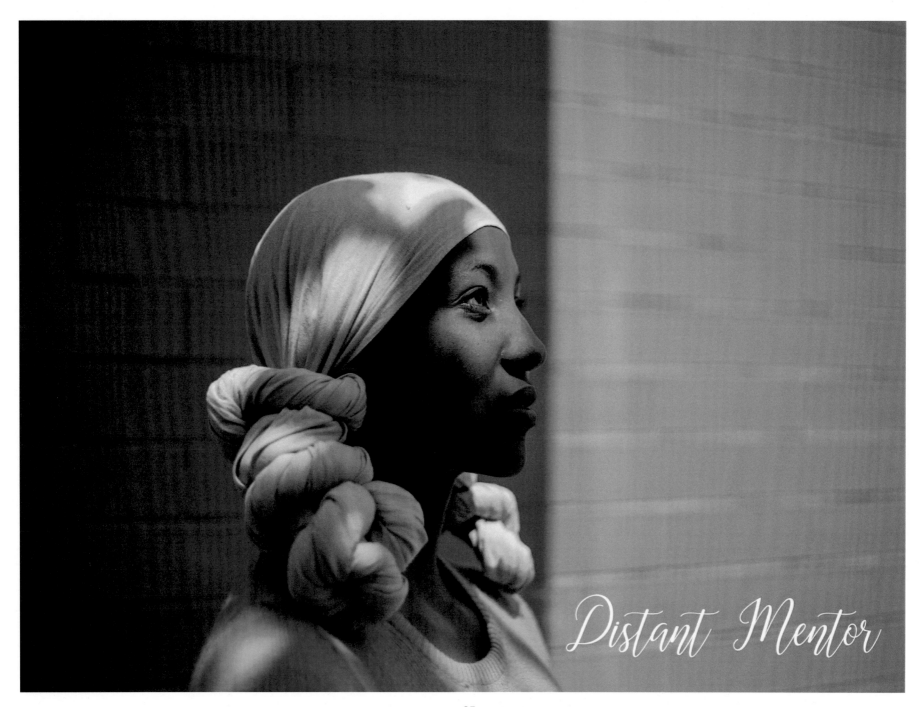

Distant Mentor

"Distant Mentor"

Distant Mentor

Your spirit is influential to my life

I have observed the level of dignity you uphold yourself to

This mental footnote has brought about change to my existence

Placing my concentration on ME

Pursuing my dreams

Expressing my thoughts, my feelings and discovering the woman who I am to be

You bring out the poetry and love songs deep within me

You take me higher and motivate my spirit to prevail

You awaken my cores desire to improve and excel

Your love and amity are my hearts mission to achieve

As I continue to elevate through this journey

I give credit to my grandmother and GOD for raising me

However

What my mother and father were not around to teach me

And what life experiences had not yet revealed to me

You filled in the cavities

I consider you relevant to my past, present, and future

You stimulate me to learn, and pursue higher degrees

You impel me to explore through early history

Just to discover new words that define and describe what you mean to me

You sway me to study immensely

Absorb new tongues and speak new languages

Swahili in verity

I relish the journey of knowledge, wisdom and understanding

The experience of you is empowering

Distant Mentor

You inspire me

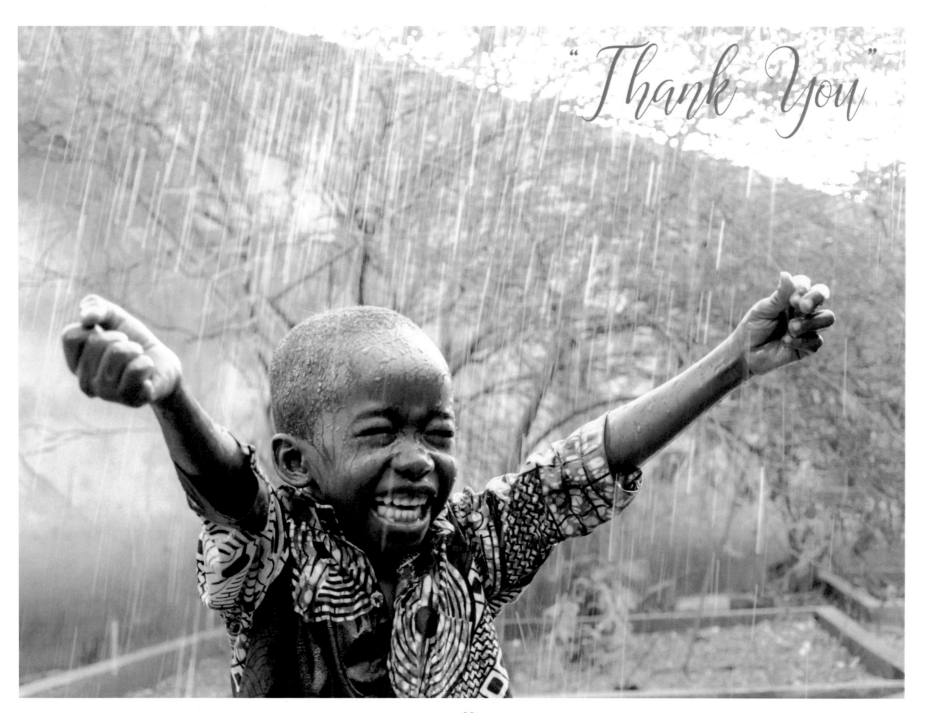

"Thank You"

89

"Thank You"

Thank you, God

For raining your love down upon me

I am grateful

For the words, visions, dreams, wisdom, knowledge

And Love's incomparable experience

Without you Lord

Letters to Love would not be possible

Thank you, Spirit

For pouring down the strength and courage to move forward with this project

Thank you, Devine Mother

For walking with me, guiding me, teaching me

Thank you, Ancestors

For the many blessings placed along my path and within my heart

I love you God

Forevermore

Amen

Ase'

Acknowledgments

This book of poetry would not have been possible without the grace and strategic plan of God. Every experience, lesson, vision, idea, and word were allowed and given to me by God in order to bring this book into fruition. I am thankful. I give thanks to my family and friends for their support and encouragement. I am thankful for those close and distant relationships that have remained steadfast no matter where we are in the world, you are appreciated. I want to give thanks to all the teachers, coaches, and athletes I was blessed to be able to mentor and work with over the past 22 years, I wish you all the best throughout your future endeavours. My heart is warm and overflowing with love and gratitude for my grandmother Ola Mae who raised me. I am graciously blessed due to her love, guidance, and abundance of prayers. I am thankful for her spirit and continuous presence within my life. I would also like to express my appreciation to my grandmothers' faithful friend Karen Haynes for always being so kind, supportive and keeping my family held up in prayer. Be blessed, I am grateful.

Sending much love, respect and appreciation to the following artist for their time, gifts, talents and contribution to this book; WillHinesPGD- *"As I Stand"* (Photo), *"Innovative Design"* (Graphics), *"Phenomenal Woman"* (Graphics), *"Dime in Disguise"* (Graphics). Author- *"Breath of Fresh Air"* (Photo), *"Innovative Design"* (Graphics), *"Phenomenal Woman"* (Graphics), *"Dime in Disguise"* (Graphics). Photo Credits: Kdshutterman- *"Living Waters,"* Yakobchuk Olena- *"Black Is Beautiful,"* Stanislav- *"Healing,"* Mimagephotos- *"Silence,"* Cincinart - Front cover & *"Innovative Design,"* Shangarey - Front Cover, Table of Contents & *"Innovative Design,"* Svetlanamiku- *"Queen of Elegance,"* BONNINSTUDIO/Stocksy- *"Welcoming You,"* Zinkevych- *"Communication,"* Poco_bw- *"King,"* Luengo_ua- *"You,"* Goldnetz & Terryleewhite - *"Phenomenal Woman,"* Redhorst- *"Sweet Taste of Love,"* Erickson Stock – *"When I'm Around You,"* Streetflash- *"Wisdom,"* NinaMalyna- *"Unforgettable,"* Viacheslav Iakobchuk- *"Love Language,"* Jbrown- *"Pass the Baton,"* Drobot Dean- *"Great Times,"* DavidPrado- *"I Try Not to Think of You"* & *"While at Rest,"* Monkey Business- *"One,"* Vagengeym- *"Love Is Impeccable,"* Zolotareva_elina & Vladimirfloyd- *"Dime in Disguise,"* Stockyimages- *"Bold & Beautiful,"* Zolotareva_elina- *"Prayer,"* Diversity Photos- *"Let Me Be the One,"* Mimagephotos- *"I'm Ready,"* Riccardo Niels Mayer- *"Thank You,"* Annatamila- *"As I go through Life,"* Elise Mesner- *"Step into the Light,"* Amaal Said- *"Distant Mentor,"* Emotionpicture- *"The Process,"* Felina B. Flossin of Flossy Flicks Photography- *Author Photo*, and SFR Beats- *"Jilly"* instrumental for promotional video.

I want to acknowledge and give special thanks to Kiki Wasp, Kimiko Walton, Kanika A. Vann, Djuana Dickerson, Cicely Smith, William Hines Jr, and Michael Abrams, for all the good times, loyalty, laughter, and support. Last, but certainly not least, I give thanks for the incomparable experience of Love. I thank you Love for being my greatest teacher, elevating my mind, filling my heart, demonstrating understanding, forgiveness, and strength. Most importantly, I appreciate and acknowledge the energy of Love as my soul's inspiration throughout this journey.

It is my soul's intention to freely share and spread LOVE throughout the world.

Peace & Blessings!